WHAT THE **BIBLE** SAYS ABOUT

HEAVEN & ETERNITY

WHAT THE **BIBLE** SAYS ABOUT

HEAVEN & ETERNITY

THOMAS ICE
TIMOTHY J. DEMY
REVISED EDITION

kregel
PUBLICATIONS

Grand Rapids, MI 49501

What the Bible Says About Heaven & Eternity

© 1997, 2000 by Thomas Ice and Timothy J. Demy
Second Edition

Previously published as *The Truth about Heaven and Eternity.*

Published by Kregel Publications, a division of Kregel, Inc.,
P.O. Box 2607, Grand Rapids, MI 49501. Kregel Publications
provides trusted, biblical publications for Christian growth and
service. Your comments and suggestions are valued. For more
information about Kregel Publications, visit our web page:
http://www.kregel.com

Unless otherwise noted, Scripture quotations are from the *New
American Standard Bible.* © the Lockman Foundation 1960,
1962, 1963, 1968, 1971, 1972, 1973, 1975, 1977.

Scripture quotations marked NKJV are from *The New King James
Version.* © 1979, 1980, 1982, Thomas Nelson, Inc., Publishers.

Scripture quotations marked KJV are from the King James
version of the Holy Bible.

All views expressed in this work are solely those of the authors and do not represent or reflect the position or endorse-
ment of any governmental agency or department, military or
otherwise.

ISBN 0-8254-2903-x

Printed in the United States of America

1 2 3 4 5 / 04 03 02 01 00

CONTENTS

PREFACE

What the Bible Says About Heaven & Eternity is designed to provide readers a brief summary of this prophetic topic. So that it can be used for quick reference or during short periods of time, this work is written in a question-and-answer format. The questions follow a logical progression so that those reading straight through will receive a greater appreciation for the topic and the issues involved. Thorough, though not exhaustive, this title is fully documented and contains a bibliography for further reading for those who desire to pursue this topic in greater depth.

The theological perspective presented throughout this title is that of premillennialism and pretribulationism. The authors recognize that this view is not the only position embraced by evangelical Christians, but we believe that it is the most widely held and prominent perspective. It is also our conviction that premillennialism, and specifically pretribulationism, *best* explains the prophetic plan of God as revealed in the Bible.

The study of prophecy and its puzzling pieces is a detailed and complex endeavor, but it is not beyond comprehension or resolution. It is open to error, misinterpretation, and confusion. Such possibilities should not, however, cause any Christian to shy away from either the study of prophecy or engagement in honest and open discussions about it. The goal of this book is to provide a concise and consistent tool for everyone who desires to understand the Scriptures better. If you will do the digging, the rewards will be great and the satisfaction will remain with you as you grow in your knowledge and love of our Lord Jesus Christ and His Word.

INTRODUCTION

In ages past, in the midst of suffering and death, Job asked, "If a man dies, will he live again?" (Job 14:14). Centuries passed before there was the sure and final answer given by Jesus Christ, who said in John 11:25–26, "I am the resurrection and the life; he who believes in Me shall live even if he dies and everyone who lives and believes in Me shall never die" (NASB). On the eve of His crucifixion, Jesus told the disciples, "In My Father's house are many dwelling places; if it were not so, I would have told you; for I go to prepare a place for you. And if I go and prepare a place for you, I will come again, and receive you to Myself; that where I am, there you may be also" (John 14:2–3).

The place of which Jesus spoke is heaven. It is the hope of all who believe in Him. Throughout the centuries, heaven has been depicted by artists and poets, authors and preachers. Augustine, Dante, John Milton, John Bunyan, C. S. Lewis, and scores of others have written on heaven and its glories. It is sung about in hymns, spirituals, classical music, and country and western music. It is spoken of in jokes and in sermons, in hospitals and in classrooms. Almost everyone has some vague notions about it, some of them biblical and some of them unbiblical. The promise of heaven has brought hope to the weary, comfort to the grieving, and reassurance to those struggling in spiritual battles.

Heaven is very real. In an age of fantasy, special effects, mysticism, and spiritual apathy, it's easy for heaven to be misrepresented. Yet, the Bible is very clear about the existence and purpose of heaven. Heaven and the eternal state are part of God's plan for the ages; therefore, heaven and prophecy are integrally related.

Sometimes, the most significant news in the newspaper is found not on the front page or in the headlines but in the obituaries. If we have not already been notified by friends and loved ones, it is there that we learn of the death of friends, neighbors, and acquaintances. These brief lines and columns remind us of the brevity of life and the certainty of death. When we think about our own death or the death of a loved one or friend, theology becomes very personal.

What we believe about life and death, good and evil, and heaven and hell is most significant. C. S. Lewis wrote of heaven's importance, noting, "If you read history, you will find that the Christians who did most for the present world were just those who thought most of the next. . . . It is because Christians have largely ceased to think of the other world that they have become so ineffective in this one."[1] How true that is for all of us! When we think about heaven, it is of the utmost personal and theological significance.

Eschatology is the theological study of future events based upon Bible prophecy. All of the biblical prophecies regarding the future will be fulfilled according to God's plan and timing. Eschatology is about future events and personalities. It also relates to every person who has lived, is living, or will live. The Bible's teaching about heaven and hell relate to what we might term "personal eschatology." Heaven and hell are very real and very personal. They relate to your future.

Pastor and author Steven J. Lawson has written the following of heaven:

> Make no mistake about it, Heaven is a *real* place. It is not a state of mind. Not a figment of man's imagination. Not a philosophical concept. Not a religious abstraction. Not a sentimental dream. Not the medieval fancy of an ancient scientist. Not the worn-out superstition of a liberal theologian. It's an actual place. A location far more real than where you presently live. . . . It is a *real* place where God lives. It is the *real* place from which Christ came

into this world. And it is the *real* place to which Christ
returned at His ascension—*really!*[2]

The Bible doesn't tell us everything we would like to know
about heaven, but it does tell some things. It gives us glimpses of
the future to encourage us in the present. Let's see what the
Bible teaches about heaven—the glorious future that awaits all
Christians.

PART 1

WHAT IS HEAVEN?

1. Where does the Bible teach about heaven?

English translations of the Bible contain more than five hundred occurrences of the word *heaven*. Most of the verses use either the Hebrew word *shamayim,* which is literally translated "the heights," or the Greek word *ouranos,* which is literally translated "that which is raised up." These words are used throughout the Bible to refer to three different locations or realms: the atmosphere, the universe, and the abode of God. These three divisions have been recognized throughout history in both Christian and non-Christian sources, especially in classical Greek literature.[1] Although our concern is primarily the third usage, all three usages are common in the Bible.

- *The atmospheric heaven.* Examples of this usage are seen in passages such as Deuteronomy 11:11, 17; 28:12, 24; Joshua 10:11; Psalms 18:13; 147:8; Proverbs 23:5; and Zechariah 2:6; 6:5. Verses such as these emphasize the "first heaven," or the atmospheric realm. It is of this realm that Isaiah speaks when he records God's words in Isaiah 55:9–11:

  For as the heavens are higher than the earth, so are My ways higher than your ways, and My thoughts than your thoughts. For as the rain and the snow come down from heaven, and do not return there without watering the earth, and making it bear and sprout, and furnishing seed to the sower and bread to the eater; so shall My word be which goes forth from My mouth; it shall not return to Me empty, without accomplishing what I desire, and without succeeding in the matter for which I sent it.

- *The universe or celestial skies.* Examples of this usage are seen in passages such as Genesis 1:14; 15:5; Exodus 20:4; Psalm 33:6; Jeremiah 10:2; and Hebrews 1:10. Frequently, the celestial skies or heavens are used biblically in a figure of speech such as a hyperbole (Deut. 1:28; Dan. 4:11, 20, 22) or a metonymy, which emphasizes totality (Deut. 4:39; 30:19; Matt. 24:31; Col. 1:23). It is of this realm of the celestial skies and the totality of the universe that we read in Deuteronomy 30:19:

  > I call heaven and earth to witness against you today, that I have set before you life and death, the blessing and the curse. So choose life in order that you may live, you and your descendants. . . .

  It is also in this sense that we read of Jesus Christ's authority in Matthew 28:18–20:

  > And Jesus came up and spoke to them, saying, "All authority has been given to Me in heaven and on earth. Go therefore and make disciples of all the nations, baptizing them in the name of the Father and the Son and the Holy Spirit, teaching them to observe all that I commanded you; and lo, I am with you always, even to the end of the age."

- *The abode of God.* Examples of this usage are the primary focus of this study and are seen in passages such as Psalm 33:13–14; Isaiah 63:15; Matthew 5:16, 45; 6:1, 9; 7:11, 21; 18:10; and Revelation 3:12; 21:10. It is the abode of God that Jesus speaks of when He stated in Matthew 10:32–33:

  > Every one therefore who shall confess Me before men, I will also confess him before My Father who is in heaven. But whoever shall deny Me before men, I will also deny him before My Father who is in heaven.

It is the abode of God, the "third heaven" of which Paul speaks in 2 Corinthians 12:2. Jesus referred to heaven in this sense many times throughout His ministry. It is also of this usage that Paul writes throughout his letters to the early churches.

Heaven is more than a mystical notion, an imaginary dreamland, or a philosophical concept. It is a real and present place in which God, the Creator of all things, lives. It is a place spoken of throughout the Bible. It is the true home of all Christians. It is from where Jesus came at the Incarnation, where He ascended after the Resurrection, and from whence He will come again to receive all of those who truly follow Him. It is the place that the writer of Hebrews calls a "distant country" and for which those in his "hall of faith" longed:

> All these died in faith, without receiving the promises, but having seen them and having welcomed them from a distance, and having confessed that they were strangers and exiles on the earth. For those who say such things make it clear that they are seeking a country of their own. And indeed if they had been thinking of that *country* from which they went out, they would have had opportunity to return. But as it is, they desire a better *country,* that is a heavenly one. Therefore God is not ashamed to be called their God; for He has prepared a city for them. (11:13–16)

2. Is there any difference between heaven and eternity?

When we talk about heaven, we are referring to a location or place. When we speak of eternity, we are talking about an era or eternal state. Heaven exists now even though we are not experiencing it. The eternal state is a yet-future dimension of time (without end). Heaven exists now and will continue to exist throughout eternity.

3. Where is heaven, and does it exist now?

The apostle Paul, writing to us as Christians in Philippians 3:20, says that "our citizenship is in heaven." Heaven is somewhere beyond earth and our universe. Heaven is in existence now and has been the dwelling place of God since eternity past. Heaven is the dwelling place of God, although God is not limited spatially to heaven because He is omnipresent. His omnipresence is reflected in Solomon's prayer at the dedication of the temple. "Behold, heaven and the highest heaven cannot contain Thee, how much less this house which I have built!" (1 Kings 8:27).

In Psalm 139:8, the psalmist also speaks of God's omnipresence, stating, "If I ascend to heaven, Thou art there; if I make my bed in Sheol, behold, Thou art there." God's omnipresence does not limit Him to heaven, but heaven is His habitation. John MacArthur writes,

> So to say that God dwells in heaven is not to say that He is contained there. But it is uniquely His home, His center of operations, His command post. It is the place where His throne resides. And it's where the most perfect worship of Him occurs. It is in that sense that we say heaven is His dwelling-place.[2]

Although heaven is a place, it is not limited by physical boundaries or boundaries of time and space. It can be experienced and inhabited by beings with material bodies, but it is not restricted to things such as height and width and breadth.[3] It has physical characteristics and attributes, but it is also extra-physical. MacArthur writes of heaven's attributes and uniqueness:

> So heaven is not confined to one locality marked off by boundaries that can be seen or measured. It transcends the confines of time-space dimensions. Perhaps that is part of what Scripture means when it states that God inhabits eternity (Isa. 57:15). His dwelling-place—heaven—is not subject to normal limitations of finite dimensions. We don't need to speculate about *how* this can be; it is sufficient to note that this is how Scripture describes heaven. It is a real place where people with physical bodies will dwell in God's presence for all eternity; and it is also a realm that surpasses our finite concept of what a "place" is.[4]

Although it is very real, heaven may be nonspatial in its present intermediate state. It is the place where Christ is now, but it is also beyond our normal senses and experiences. It is truly a supernatural phenomenon.[5]

4. When does the eternal state or eternity begin?

According to Revelation 21 and 22, the eternal state will begin at the end of the Millennium, the thousand-year reign of Christ on earth. From our current point in history, the next event in God's prophetic plan is the Rapture of the church, which will be followed by the seven-year Tribulation, the second coming of Christ, the millennial kingdom, and finally, the eternal state.

Eternity is distinct from the millennial kingdom. During the Millennium, Jesus Christ will rule on earth for one thousand years. At the end of this period, there will be a series of judgments and the ushering in of the eternal state.

5. What is the eternal city?

After the judgments at the end of the Millennium, Jerusalem and the rest of the earth will be destroyed by fire (Matt. 24:35; 2 Peter 3:10). However, according to Revelation 3:12 and 21–22, there will be a new city, the New Jerusalem, which will replace the destroyed city and which will continue throughout eternity. This new Jerusalem is the "eternal city."

Jesus told His disciples in John 14:2–3 that He was going away to heaven to prepare a place for believers. It appears that this place that He is preparing is the heavenly Jerusalem.

The New Jerusalem will be a heavenly city throughout eternity in that its origin is heavenly, as opposed to having been built upon this earth. However, it will be earthly, in that it is physical and geographical, and it will be the earthly part of the new heavens and the new earth that will replace the current heavens and earth after their destruction. After this present earth has been destroyed by fire (2 Peter 3:10), then the new city will descend from the heavens.

> And I saw a new heaven and a new earth; for the first heaven and the first earth passed away, and there is no longer any

sea. And I saw the holy city, new Jerusalem, coming down out of heaven from God, made ready as a bride adorned for her husband. And I heard a loud voice from the throne, saying, "Behold, the tabernacle of God is among men, and He shall dwell among them, and they shall be His people, and God Himself shall be among them." (Revelation 21:1-3)

Revelation 21-22 is very specific and detailed about the city, its inhabitants, and the blessedness of the eternal state. Although we might have many questions about eternity, John's vision leaves no doubt that citizens of this New Jerusalem, *the* Eternal City, will exist in conditions unlike any that this world has known.

6. What is the relationship between the Millennium and heaven?

The Millennium and the eternal state are two separate phases of the kingdom of God. The Millennium precedes the eternal state. Arnold Fruchtenbaum writes:

> The millennium itself is only one thousand years long. However, according to the promises of the Davidic Covenant, there was to be an eternal dynasty, an eternal kingdom and an eternal throne. The eternal existence of the dynasty is assured because it culminates in an eternal person: the Lord Jesus Christ. But the eternal existence of the throne and kingdom must also be assured. The millennial form of the kingdom of God will end after one thousand years. But the kingdom of God in the sense of God's rule will continue into the Eternal Order. Christ will continue His position of authority on the Davidic throne into the Eternal Order.[6]

The Millennium is the precursor of the eternal state. It will be different than life as we know it today, but it will still fall short of the absolute perfection of the eternal state. We read in Revelation 21-22:5 that the eternal state will entail the passing away of the old order and the creation of the New Jerusalem and new heavens and earth.

When studying the two periods of time, we observe the following contrasts.

- The Millennium is associated with the continuum of human history whereas the eternal state is not.
- The Millennium is the apex of human history because sin is still present though restrained through Christ's rule whereas heaven in the eternal state is totally void of all sin.
- The Millennium will focus worship on Jesus Christ, the second person of the Trinity whereas during the eternal state direct fellowship with God the Father, the first person of the Trinity, will be a reality for the first time in history.
- The Millennium will be a time during which resurrected believers and nonresurrected humans will routinely commingle in history whereas the eternal state will consist of only resurrected people.
- The Millennium will still be a time in history when humans come into existence and will trust or reject Christ as their Savior whereas the eternal state will be a time during which no one else will ever be added to the human race and everyone's destiny will be frozen, locked into their condition as saved or lost for eternity.

The Millennium and the eternal state will have many differences, but both of them will differ greatly from our current historical era.

7. What happens at the end of the Millennium?

At the end of the thousand-year reign of Christ on earth, there will be one final rebellion by Satan and his forces. Just as is prophesied in Revelation 20, Satan will be loosed at the end of the Millennium and will rebel against the millennial reign of Christ:

> And when the thousand years are completed, Satan will be released from his prison, and will come out to deceive the nations which are in the four corners of the earth, Gog and Magog, to gather them together for the war; the number of them is like the sand of the seashore. And they came up on

the broad plain of the earth and surrounded the camp of the saints and the beloved city, and fire came down from heaven and devoured them. And the devil who deceived them was thrown into the lake of fire and brimstone, where the beast and the false prophet are also; and they will be tormented day and night forever and ever. (Revelation 20:7–10)

In one final grasp for power and human allegiance, Satan will manifest his true nature (as he has done throughout all of history) and attempt to seize the throne of God.[7] John Walvoord writes of this attempted *coup d'état:*

The thousand years of confinement will not change Satan's nature, and he will attempt to take the place of God and receive the worship and obedience that is due God alone. He will find a ready response on the part of those who have made a profession of following Christ in the Millennium but who now show their true colors. They will surround Jerusalem in an attempt to capture the capital city of the kingdom of David as well as of the entire world. The Scriptures report briefly, "But fire came down from heaven and devoured them."[8]

According to Revelation 20:10, Satan's termination will be swift but everlasting. He will be cast into the lake of fire, joining the Antichrist and the false prophet, who is the Antichrist's lieutenant (Rev. 13:11–18). The fact that the Antichrist and the false prophet are placed into the lake of fire at the Second Coming, before the Millennium, demonstrates the fact that they are finished in history. The lake of fire is the final form of hell from which no one, once placed there, ever leaves. This is why Satan is bound in the bottomless pit at the start of the Millennium, because he will make one more appearance upon the stage of history before he is once and for all consigned to the lake of fire.

The judgment of Satan is then followed by the judgment of the unbelieving dead, known as the Great White Throne judgment (Rev. 20:11–15). These judgments form the bridge between the

Millennium and the eternal state as described in Revelation 21–22. They are the final events of the Millennium and conclude with the passing away of the present heavens and earth (Matt. 24:35; Mark 13:31; Luke 16:17; 21:33; 2 Peter 3:10). John writes,

> And I saw a new heaven and a new earth; for the first heaven and the first earth passed away, and there is no longer any sea. (Revelation 21:1)

8. How do the future judgments relate to heaven?

According to God's prophetic plan and timetable, several judgments are yet in the future. Some of these judgments will occur before and at the end of the Tribulation, and others will come at the end of the Millennium and before the eternal state. Just before the inauguration of the eternal state and the dwelling of believers in heaven for eternity, there will be the judgment of Satan and the fallen angels (Matt. 25:4; 2 Peter 2:4; Jude 6; Rev. 20:10) and the Great White Throne judgment of the unsaved that is described in Revelation 20:11–15. Charles Ryrie summarizes this final judgment thus:

> Those judged are simply called "the dead"—unbelievers (in contrast to "the dead in Christ" which refers to believers). This judgment will not separate believers from unbelievers, for all who will experience it will have made the choice during their lifetimes to reject God. The Book of Life which will be opened at the Great White Throne judgment will not contain the name of anyone who will be in that judgment. The books of works which will also be opened will prove that all who are being judged deserve eternal condemnation (and may be used to determine degrees of punishment). It is not that all their works were evil, but all were dead works, done by spiritually dead people. It is as if the Judge will say, "I will show you by the record of your own deeds that you deserve condemnation." So everyone who will appear in this judgment will be cast into the lake of fire forever.[9]

The various judgments are portrayed in the following chart. Note that all of the judgments occur before the eternal state.[10]

Judgment	Time	Place	Persons	Basis	Results	Scripture
Believers' works	Between Rapture and Second Coming	*Bema* of Christ	Believers in Christ	Works and walk of the Christian life	Rewards or loss of rewards	1 Cor. 3:10–15; 2 Cor. 5:10
Old Testament saints	End of Tribulation/ Second Coming		Believers in Old Testament times	Faith in God	Rewards	Dan. 12:1–3
Tribulation saints	End of Tribulation/ Second Coming		Believers of Tribulation period	Faith in and faithfulness to Christ	Reign with Christ in the Millennium	Rev. 20:4–6
Living Jews	End of Tribulation/ Second Coming	Wilderness	Jews who survive the Tribulation	Faith in Christ	Believers enter kingdom; rebels are purged	Ezek. 20:34–38
Living Gentiles	End of Tribulation/ Second Coming	Valley of Jehoshaphat	Gentiles who survive the Tribulation	Faith in Christ as proved by works	Believers enter the kingdom; others go to lake of fire	Joel 3:1–2; Matt. 25:31–46
Satan and fallen angels	End of Millennium	Before the Great White Throne	Satan and those angels who follow him	Allegiance to Satan's counterfeit system	Lake of fire	Matt. 25:41; 2 Peter 2:4; Jude 6; Rev. 20:10
Unsaved people	End of Millennium		Unbelievers of all time	Rejection to God	Lake of fire	Rev. 20:11–15

End-Time Judgments

PART 2

WHAT WILL HEAVEN BE LIKE?

9. What will take place in heaven?

The Bible describes life in heaven as full of joy, purposeful activity, and worship. When we think of eternity, it's easy to wonder if we will get bored in heaven. However, the biblical glimpses are not of boredom. The Bible speaks of at least six activities in heaven: worship, service, authority and administration, fellowship, learning, and rest.[1]

- *Worship without distraction.* Worship will be the primary activity in heaven. "Perhaps the first great and continuous activity for the redeemed will be worship of the triune God."[2] Some of the most extensive passages on worship in heaven are found in Revelation 4–5 and 19:1–8.

  "Worship will no longer be an indefinable word or an indescribable experience. It will not be manipulated or contrived. All its pretense lost, worship will be one of the first and great continuous activities of the redeemed. It will be spontaneous and genuine. It will encompass the whole universe. The *hallelujahs* and the *praise the Lords* and the *amens* will drown out all of the sounds of Heaven and earth, and we will all lose ourselves in the joy of telling our God how much we adore Him."[3] On the basis of Revelation 4:8–11, the worship of God in heaven can be seen to include at least six things:[4]

  A celebration of God's greatness (v. 8).
  A celebration of God's goodness (v. 9).
  A submission before God's sovereignty (v. 10).
  An adoration of God's person (v. 10).

A self-renunciation before God's glory (v. 10).
An exaltation of God's name (v. 11).

- *Service without exhaustion.* In Revelation 22:3 we read, "And there shall no longer be any curse; and the throne of God and of the Lamb shall be in it, and His bond-servants shall serve Him." Throughout Revelation, the phrase *bond-servant* is used to describe those who are in heaven and experiencing its glories. Unlike the current work, future service to God in heaven will be without time demands, without frustration, without fear of failure, without limitations, and without exhaustion. It will come from worship and motivation that is pure, and it will be a joyful experience.

- *Administration without failure.* In Revelation 22:5, we read that believers in heaven shall "reign forever and ever." In Luke 19:17, 19, Jesus taught that in the future reward and authority would be given to those who followed Him. He also indicated that the authority and administration would include judgment over the twelve tribes of Israel (Matt. 19:28; Luke 22:30). In 1 Corinthians 6:3, Paul states that Christians will also have authority over the angels in heaven.

- *Fellowship without suspicion.* Heaven will provide believers of all ages with the opportunity for limitless fellowship with each other and with Jesus Christ (Matt. 8:11; Rev. 19:9). In heaven we will fellowship with both those Christians we knew on earth and Old Testament saints and those Christians who lived before and after us, or with those whom present circumstances have not allowed us to know.

- *Learning without weariness.* "We will not know everything in Heaven, for only God is omniscient, but will have a limitless capacity to learn. In the Fall, a curtain was lowered, which has caused us to 'see through a glass darkly,' but in Heaven that curtain will be lifted, and 'I shall know, even as I am known' [1 Cor. 13:12]. One of the great joys of Heaven will be that of taking all the time necessary to unravel all the mysteries about God, about man, and about the universe."[5]

- *Rest without boredom.* Revelation 14:10–13 contrasts the eternal destiny of the righteous and the unrighteous. In verse 11, the unrighteous are said to have "no rest" in contrast to the righteous, who will "rest from their labors, for their deeds follow with them" (v. 13). "A glorified spiritual body will know nothing of fatigue or exhaustion, so the continuing rest that God promises will not be a rest from work but a rest from want."[6] In heaven, we will be fully satisfied, and the words of David the psalmist will be fully realized by those who are God's own: "As for me, I shall behold Thy face in righteousness; I will be satisfied with Thy likeness when I awake" (Ps. 17:15).

10. Will we have bodies in heaven?

In heaven, we will have recognizable spiritual bodies just like Jesus Christ had after the Resurrection. In 1 John 3:2, the apostle John writes, "We know that, when He appears, we shall be like Him, because we shall see Him just as He is." Earlier, in his Gospel, John recorded Jesus' words regarding the resurrection of believers and the resurrection of judgment for unbelievers. He said, "An hour is coming, in which all who are in the tombs shall hear His voice, and shall come forth; those who did the good deeds to a resurrection of life, those who committed the evil deeds to a resurrection of judgment" (John 5:28–29).

The bodies that we will have in heaven will be our own earthly bodies glorified. They will have the same qualities as the glorified resurrection body of Jesus Christ. According to Philippians 3:21, Jesus Christ "will transform the body of our humble state into conformity with the body of His glory, by the exertion of the power that He has even to subject all things to Himself." In our resurrection bodies, the effects of the Fall and of sin will be removed. The bodies will be real but without the physical limitations that we now experience and without the effects of disease, disability, or tragedy. Author and artist Joni Eareckson Tada, who became a quadriplegic after a diving accident as a teenager, writes of the certainty and glory of our resurrected bodies as described in 1 Corinthians 15:

Somewhere in my broken, paralyzed body is the seed of what I shall become. The paralysis makes what I am to become all the more grand when you contrast atrophied, useless legs against splendorous resurrected legs. I'm convinced that if there are mirrors in heaven (and why not?), the image I'll see will be unmistakably "Joni," although a much better, brighter "Joni." So much so, that it's not worth comparing. . . . I will bear the likeness of Jesus, the man from heaven. Like His, mine will be an actual, literal body perfectly suited for earth *and* heaven. . . . We shall be perfectly fitted for our environment, whether it be the new heavens or new earth.[7]

All believers, regardless of the cause or nature of their death or the disposition of their remains at death, will miraculously receive new bodies. According to 1 Corinthians 15, our bodies will be imperishable, glorious, powerful, and spiritual. John MacArthur writes,

All this is to say that in heaven we will have real bodies that are permanently and eternally perfect. You will never look in a mirror and notice wrinkles or a receding hairline. You will never have a day of sickness. You won't be susceptible to injury, or disease, or allergies. There will be none of those things in heaven. There will only be absolute, imperishable perfection.[8]

The doctrine of bodily resurrection and glorified bodies is essential to orthodoxy and the Christian message (1 Cor. 15:35–36). Based on the testimony and promises of the Bible, it is the great and glorious hope of Christians throughout all ages that they will one day be united with Jesus Christ in heavenly bodies. It is of this hope that Paul speaks in 1 Corinthians 15:12–19:

Now if Christ is preached, that He has been raised from the dead, how do some among you say that there is no resurrection of the dead? But if there is no resurrection of the dead, not even Christ has been raised; and if Christ has not been raised, then our preaching is vain, your faith also is vain. Moreover we are even found to be false witnesses of God, because we witnessed against God that He raised Christ whom He did not raise, if in fact the dead are not raised. For if the dead are not raised, not even Christ has been raised; and if Christ has not been raised, your faith is worthless; you are still in your sins. Then those also who have fallen asleep in Christ have perished. If we have only hoped in Christ in this life, we are of all men most to be pitied.

11. Will we have personal identity and recognize others in heaven?

When we get to heaven, we will clearly recognize others. When He was in His resurrection body, Jesus was clearly and readily recognized. In this same manner, we will be known and recognized by each other in heaven. We will not be nameless and faceless souls without identities. Rather, we will maintain our current identities but in resurrected and glorified bodies that have no infirmities or faults.

At the Last Supper, Jesus promised the disciples that in the millennial kingdom and in heaven they would all drink the fruit of the vine together again as they did that evening (Matt. 8:11; Luke 22:17–18). John MacArthur writes,

All the redeemed will maintain their identity forever, but in a perfected form. We will be able to have fellowship with Enoch, Noah, Abraham, Jacob, Samuel, Moses, Joshua, Esther, Elijah, Elisha, Isaiah, Daniel, Ezekiel, David, Peter, Barnabas, Paul, or any of the saints we choose.

Remember that Moses and Elijah appeared with Christ on the Mount of Transfiguration. Even though they died centuries before, they still maintained a clear identity (Matt. 17:3). Moreover, Peter, James, and John evidently recognized them (v. 4)—which implies that we will somehow be able to recognize people we've never even seen before. For that to be possible, we must all retain our individual identities, not turn into some sort of generic beings.[9]

12. Will we be reunited with Christian family members and friends in heaven?

One of the greatest heartaches we face in this world is the longing and desire for loved ones and friends who are deceased. The desire to be with them and share our intimate concerns, thoughts, and wants is very real and strong. For Christians, such a reunion will happen in heaven and it will be an eternal reunion. Those whom we knew and loved for years or decades on earth will be with us for eternity.

In Psalm 116:15, we read, "Precious in the sight of the LORD is the death of His godly ones." God brings into His presence all of the redeemed, and each one is dear to Him, even more so than they are to us. We can be assured that in heaven we will know them, join them, and love them even more than we did here on earth. Although friends and family might grieve for them now, we will not always, for God "shall wipe away every tear from their eyes; and there shall no longer be any death; there shall no longer be any mourning, or crying, or pain; the first things have passed away" (Rev. 21:4).

13. Is there marriage in heaven?

It is natural for us to wonder about the nature of our relationships with others in heaven, especially those who are close or intimate, such as families, dear friends, and spouses.

The Bible clearly teaches that although our relationships will be perfect in heaven, there will be no marriage. In 1 Corinthians 7:29–31, the apostle Paul writes that the *form* (literally "schema" from the Greek) of this world is passing away. The relationships of this world and the way or manner of life, including marriage, will one day no longer exist.

> But this I say, brethren, the time has been shortened, so that from now on both those who have wives should be as though they had none; and those who weep, as though they did not weep; and those who rejoice, as though they did not rejoice; and those who buy, as though they did not possess; and those who use the world, as though they did

not make full use of it; for the *form* of this world is passing away.

John MacArthur writes of this passage and our relationships in heaven:

> Paul is not questioning the legitimacy of earthly blessings such as marriage, normal human emotions, and earthly ownership. But he is saying that we must never allow our emotions and possessions to control us so that we become entangled in this passing world. . . . Concentrate on the things of the Lord, because marriage is only a temporary provision.
>
> If you're already married, however, this does not mean you may become indifferent to your marriage. Too much elsewhere in Scripture elevates the importance of marriage and commands husbands and wives to seek to honor God through the marriage relationship. But this passage simply underscores the temporal nature of marriage. While married couples are heirs together of the grace of *this* life (cf. 1 Peter 3:7), the institution of marriage is passing away. There are higher eternal values.[10]

When Jesus was asked about marriage in heaven and the afterlife, He taught that it was clearly a temporal union. When some Sadducees, who did not believe in the afterlife, came to Him and asked Him a question in an attempt to force Him into taking sides with either them or the Pharisees (who believed we would have the same relationships in heaven as on earth), Jesus rebuked them sharply. After listening to a hypothetical scenario regarding marriage in this life and the afterlife, Jesus responded,

> You are mistaken, not understanding the Scriptures, or the power of God. For in the resurrection they neither marry, nor are given in marriage, but are like angels in heaven. (Matthew 22:29–30)

14. How do angels relate to heaven and eternity?

Angels are very real. They exist and minister today just as they have in the past, and they will continue to exist in heaven and eternity. They are created spiritual beings (Ps. 148:5) that do not procreate (Matt. 22:30) and that function as messengers and servants of God (Heb. 1:14). Theologian and Bible scholar Charles Ryrie writes of angels:

> If one accepts the biblical revelation then there can be no question about the existence of angels. There are three significant characteristics about revelation. First, it is extensive. The Old Testament speaks about angels just over 100 times, while the New Testament mentions them about 165 times. . . .
>
> Second, angels are mentioned throughout the Bible. The truth about them is not confined to one period of history or one part of the Scriptures or a few writers. They do not belong to some primitive era. Their existence is mentioned in thirty-four books of the Bible from the earliest (whether Gen. or Job) to the last.
>
> Third, the teaching of our Lord includes a number of references to angels as real beings. So to deny their existence is to cast doubt on His veracity.[11]

Angels will participate in the prophetic events before the eternal state. Just as they were present at Christ's first coming, so also will they be present at the Rapture (1 Thess. 4:16), during the Tribulation (Rev. 8–9; 16), at the Second Coming (Matt. 25:31; 2 Thess. 1:7), and at the final judgment (Matt. 13:39–40).

Angels will be present in heaven and eternity and Christians will judge them because of our union with Christ. In 1 Corinthians 6:3, Paul tells the Corinthians, "Do you not know that we shall judge the angels?" We also know from passages such as 2 Peter 2:4 and Jude 6 that the fallen angels who sided with Satan when he rebelled against God will be judged in the future and cast into hell with him.

PART 3

WHO WILL BE IN HEAVEN?

15. Who are the occupants of heaven?

In heaven there is and will be God, angels, and redeemed believers.

- *God.* Heaven is God's dwelling place. Psalm 103:19 says, "The LORD has established His throne in the heavens; and His sovereignty rules over all."
- *Angels.* Angels are given assignments throughout the universe and have access to heaven and earth, but their home is in heaven (Dan. 7:10; Isa. 6:1–6; Mark 13:32; John 1:51).
- *Believers.* All Christians of all ages, along with the redeemed of the Old Testament era, will have their eternal home in heaven (Rev. 5:9). Philippians 3:20 states, "For our citizenship is in heaven, from which also we eagerly wait for a Savior, the Lord Jesus Christ."

Heaven will be filled eternally with those who know and love God. It will be a place of praise and worship, joy and gladness. The trials and tribulations of this world will be gone, and the true citizenship of Christians will be fully realized. John recorded a preview of heaven, God's "coming attraction," in the book of Revelation. We read there of heaven's occupants:

After these things I looked, and behold, a great multitude, which no one could count, from every nation and all tribes and peoples and tongues, standing before the throne and before the Lamb, clothed in white robes, and palm branches were in their hands; and they cry out with a loud voice, saying, "Salvation to our God who sits on the throne, and to the Lamb." And all the angels were standing around the throne and around the elders and the four living creatures; and they fell on their faces before the throne and worshipped God, saying, "Amen, blessing and glory and wisdom and thanksgiving and honor and power and might, be to our God forever and ever, Amen." (Revelation 7:9–12)

16. What happens now at the moment of death?

When a Christian dies, his or her spirit is immediately brought into heaven and the eternal presence of God. The Bible clearly teaches that when Christians die, they are instantaneously present with God. In Philippians 1:23, Paul writes, "But I am hard pressed from both directions, having the desire to depart and be with Christ, for that is very much the better." Notice that there is no indication of any time lapse in his comment. This is stated even stronger in 2 Corinthians 5:6–8, where he writes,

> Therefore, being always of good courage, and knowing that while we are at home in the body we are absent from the Lord—for we walk by faith, not by sight—we are of good courage, I say, and prefer rather to be absent from the body and to be at home with the Lord.

Hebrews 12:23 also suggests that believers who have died are now in heaven without their resurrected bodies, awaiting the time when the body and the soul will be united in a final glorified state.

Jesus clearly promised the thief who was crucified beside him that they would be together in paradise at the same moment and day (Luke 23:43). In Revelation 6:9–11, John writes of the souls of disembodied spirits martyred during the early days of the Tribulation crying out for divine justice. These verses show a consciousness of believers and their presence with God. John MacArthur writes of the death of believers:

> God made man body and soul—we consist of an inner man and an outer man (Gen. 2:7). Therefore our ultimate perfection demands that both body and soul be renewed. Even

the creation of a new heaven and new earth demands that we have bodies—a real earth calls for its inhabitants to have real bodies. . . .

Death results in separation of the body and the soul. Our bodies go to the grave, and our spirits go to the Lord. The separation continues until the resurrection: "The hour is coming, in which all that are in the graves shall hear his voice, and shall come forth; they that have done good, unto the resurrection of life; and they that have done evil, unto the resurrection of damnation" (John 5:28–29 KJV). Right now the souls of believers who have died are in heaven. But someday their bodies will be resurrected and joined to their spirits, and they will enjoy the eternal perfection of body and soul.[1]

Unbelievers are not and will not be in heaven. At the time of death, their body enters the grave, and the soul of the unbeliever enters hades to wait for the final judgment at the end of the Millennium. Like believers' bodies, the unbelievers' bodies will one day be joined with their souls, but it will be for final judgment, and they will not receive glorified bodies.

17. What about the concept of soul sleep?

Some groups, such as Seventh-Day Adventists and the Jehovah's Witnesses, teach a concept of soul sleep. This view holds that during the time interval between death and resurrection is an unconsciousness or sleep into which persons enter. The concept is based on the fact that several passages in the Bible refer to death as "sleep" (Dan. 12:2; Matt. 9:24; John 11:11; 1 Thess. 4:13–16; 5:10). We have, however, several biblical and theological objections to the doctrine and to taking these passages as referring to soul sleep.[2]

- Several passages—including Luke 23:43; 2 Corinthians 5:1–10; and Philippians 1:23—teach that death for the believer is an immediate transition into conscious enjoyment of the presence of Christ. This situation could not be so if they were in soul sleep.
- Some of these same passages refer to death as a gain because

the deceased is immediately with Christ. If the believer were in soul sleep, it would not be a gain.

- In 1 Thessalonians 5:10, Paul writes, "[Christ] died for us, that whether we are awake or asleep, we may live together with Him." If being "asleep" here means soul sleep, then the verse makes no sense; we would not then "live together with Him."

- Because sleep is an activity of the body, the soul sleeps now only because it is embodied. Once the body and the soul are separated at death, it is unclear how a disembodied soul *could* or would *need* to have rest.

- The existence of angels is proof that spirits can and do exist and have conscious, disembodied lives. Therefore, no problem exists with the concept of a conscious, disembodied intermediate state for human beings.

- The history and usage of the word *sleep* in the ancient Near Eastern, Egyptian, and Greek cultures makes arguing for soul sleep difficult because the word commonly described the appearance and posture of the body, not the soul.

Soul sleep is not a biblical doctrine, and it adds confusion to the prophetic teachings of the Bible. If soul sleep is true, then we must cast aside Scripture because we cannot, as Paul teaches, "prefer rather to be absent from the body and to be at home with the Lord" (2 Cor. 5:8).

18. Who enters heaven?

Heaven is for all those who have obtained salvation based on the death of Jesus Christ. As we have seen from the preceding questions, the souls of all believers enter heaven at the moment of death. There they await, with the Old Testament saints, their glorified resurrection bodies.

People long to live life to its fullest; yet, for Christians "the fullest" will come only after death. It will come in heaven when we see our Creator and Lord face to face and are finally and eternally "home." Ken Gire has written of our frequent misperception of death: "Death. It is the most misunderstood part of life. It is not a great sleep but a great awakening. It is that moment when we awake, rub our eyes, and see things at last the way God has seen them all along."[3]

19. What happens when infants, children, and others who can't believe in Jesus Christ die?

This issue is certainly one of the most personal, emotional, and difficult questions we face as Christians. Many people, because of diminished mental capacities or because they die as infants or young children, do not have the opportunity to respond to the offer of salvation through Jesus Christ. The Bible does not give us all of the clarity or intricacy of response that we desire in answers regarding their destiny, but it does give some assurance to us and provides several insights.

When King David's very young son died, David mourned his death but firmly believed that he would one day be reunited with his son in heaven. We read David's words in 2 Samuel 12:22–23: "While the child was still alive, I fasted and wept; for I said, 'Who knows, the LORD may be gracious to me, that the child may live.' But now he has died; why should I fast? Can I bring him back again? I shall go to him, but he will not return to me." David knew that death was inevitable, but he fully expected to be reunited with his son after death.

In Matthew 18:1–6, 10–14, and 19:14, Jesus speaks with extreme gentleness and favor regarding children and the kingdom of God. On the basis of these and other passages, the majority of Christian theologians have held to salvation for those such as infants who can't believe in Christ's redeeming work. Representative of this perspective, Ron Rhodes writes,

> It would be a cruel mockery for God to call upon infants to do—and to hold them *responsible* for doing—what they *could not* do. At a young age children simply do not have the capacity to exercise saving faith in Christ.
>
> I believe it is the uniform testimony of Scripture that those who are not capable of making a decision to receive Jesus Christ, when they die, go to be with Christ in heaven,

resting in His tender arms, enjoying the sweetness of His love.[4]

The view presented by Rhodes and many others is that if an individual dies before he or she reaches an age or capacity for moral accountability, the individual is granted salvation at the moment of death. In James 4:17, we read, "Therefore, to one who knows the right thing to do, and does not do it, to him it is sin." Rhodes writes, "It would seem, then, that when a child truly comes into a full awareness and moral understanding of 'oughts' and 'shoulds,' he or she at that point has reached the age of accountability."[5] He continues,

> Even though the child does not become morally responsible before God until this time, he or she nevertheless has a sin nature that alienates him or her from God from the moment of birth. And whatever solution a person comes up with in regard to the issue of infant salvation must deal with this problem.
>
> The solution, it seems to me, must be that at the moment the infant dies—*and not before*—the benefits of Jesus' atoning death on the cross are applied to him or her. And at that moment, the infant becomes saved and is immediately brought into the presence of God in heaven. This view is consistent not just with the love of God, but His holiness as well.[6]

Another passage used in support of the concept of the age of accountability is Revelation 20:12–13, which states that the final judgment of the wicked is "according to their deeds." Rhodes writes, "The basis of this judgment of the wicked is clearly deeds done while on earth. Hence, infants and mentally handicapped people cannot possibly be the objects of this judgment because they are not responsible for their deeds. Such a judgment against infants would be a travesty."[7]

The age of accountability is considered to extend to preborn babies as well as infants and others.[8] We know with absolute certainty that God's attributes include absolute love, justice, and goodness (Pss. 31:19; 103:6, 8–10; Nah. 1:7; Zeph. 3:5; 1 John 4:16). For those who grieve or have grieved the loss of a child or questioned the destiny of another person who is or was unable to believe, we are assured that they are more precious to God than we can imagine. He knows our fears and sees our tears and will not permit any individual or group of individuals to perish without willful choice. Robert Lightner has written appropriately, "How would God be just in refusing into His presence those who were never able to receive or reject His salvation?"[9]

20. How does Jesus Christ relate to heaven?

Forty days after the Resurrection, Jesus entered heaven, and He will remain there until the Rapture (Acts 1:9–11; 1 Thess. 4:16–17). Before His crucifixion, Jesus told the disciples that He would return to heaven to prepare an eternal home for those who believed in Him. In John 14:1–3, Jesus said,

> Let not your heart be troubled; believe in God, believe also in Me. In My Father's house are many dwelling places; if it were not so, I would have told you; for I go to prepare a place for you. And if I go and prepare a place for you, I will come again, and receive you to Myself; that where I am, there you may be also.

Believers will enjoy eternal fellowship with Jesus Christ in heaven. "Christ is the centerpiece of Heaven. All Heaven revolves around Him."[10] We will see, experience, and understand in heaven all of the glory and majesty of Christ. John MacArthur writes,

> Simply put, we're going to be with a Person as much as we are going to live in a place. The presence of Christ is what makes heaven. "The Lamb is the light thereof" (Rev. 21:23 KJV). And perfect fellowship with God is the very essence of heaven.[11]

PART 4

WHAT DOES THE FUTURE HOLD FOR NON-CHRISTIANS?

21. Doesn't everyone go to heaven?

We often hear the phrase "there are many paths to the mountain-top," implying that either all religions have equally valid claims to truth or that all of humanity will ultimately experience the same final disposition. Within Christianity, some people have claimed that everyone will receive salvation. Yet, this position of inclusivism does not have the support of the Bible and has not been the historic position of Christian orthodoxy. Passages such as Matthew 25:46; John 3:36; 2 Thessalonians 1:8–9, and numerous others clearly teach that salvation will not be experienced by everyone.[1] This is, admittedly, a difficult and emotional issue. It should, however, be a motivating factor for every Christian to share his or her faith. It is a very important matter, for eternity rests in the balance.

22. What is hell?

Hell is a place of eternal punishment and separation from God. It was created to accommodate Satan and the fallen angels who rebelled with him against God (Matt. 25:41). People who reject Jesus Christ and His free offer of salvation will join Satan in hell in eternity. Hell is a very real place of literal fire and flames, but the most important thing to know about it is that hell is separation from God. It is what people choose rather than accepting salvation through Jesus Christ. Theologian Harold O. J. Brown commented appropriately that "Hell has been called 'the most enduring monu-ment to the freedom of the will.'"[2] Similarly, C. S. Lewis wrote, "There are only two kinds of people in the end: those who say to

God, 'Thy will be done,' and those to whom God says, '*Thy* will be done.'"[3]

The concept of hell and belief in it is not popular in our society, but hell is a valid biblical doctrine. Theologians and apologists Gary Habermas and J. P. Moreland summarize hell very well:

> Hell is a place of shame, sorrow, regret, and anguish. This intense pain is not actively produced by God; he is not a cosmic torturer. Undoubtedly, anguish and torment will exist in hell. And because we will have both body and soul in the resurrected state, the anguish experienced can be both mental and physical. But the pain suffered will be due to the shame and sorrow resulting from the punishment of final, ultimate, unending banishment from God, his kingdom, and the good life for which we were created in the first place. Hell's occupants will deeply and tragically regret all they lost. As Jesus said, "For what profit is it to a man if he gains the whole world, and loses his own soul?" (Matt. 16:26 NKJV).[4]

23. Where does the Bible teach about hell?

The Bible refers to hell using several different words throughout the Old and New Testaments. Two of the clearest passages on hell in the New Testament are 2 Thessalonians 1:9 and Matthew 25:41, 46. In 2 Thessalonians 1:9, Paul writes of those who reject God: "And these will pay the penalty of eternal destruction, away from the presence of the Lord and from the glory of His power." Jesus speaks of future judgment and hell in Matthew's Gospel:

> Then He will also say to those on His left, 'Depart from Me, accursed ones, into the eternal fire which has been prepared for the devil and his angels; . . . and these will go away into eternal punishment, but the righteous into eternal life. (25:41, 46)

Following is a brief summary of the biblical words from which we get the English word *hell*.

- *Sheol.* In the Old Testament, the Hebrew word *sheol* is used to describe hell. It occurs sixty-five times and is translated by terms such as *hell, pit, grave,* and *sheol. Sheol* can have different meanings in different contexts in the Bible. It may refer to the grave (Job 17:13; Ps. 16:10; Isa. 38:10). It also means the place to which the departed go (Gen. 37:35; 42:38; Num. 16:33; Job 14:13; Ps. 55:15). Believers will be rescued from *sheol* (Pss. 16:9–11; 17:15; 49:15), but the wicked will not (Job 21:13; 24:19; Pss. 9:17; 31:17; 49:14; 55:15). The major focus of the Old Testament is on the place where the bodies of people go, not where their souls exist. The destiny of the souls of individuals in the intermediate state is not expanded upon greatly in the Old Testament. The full doctrine of eternal destiny must be rounded out with the revelation of the New Testament. But *sheol* is definitely a place of punishment (Job 24:19) and horror (Ps. 30:9).
- *Hades.* The New Testament Greek counterpart to the Hebrew term *sheol* is *hades. Hades* was originally a proper noun in Greek, the name of the Greek god of the nether world who ruled over the dead. In the New Testament, *hades* is used in two different ways. First, it can be used to describe a place when referring to punishment (Matt. 11:23; Luke 10:15; 16:32). Second, it can refer to the state of death that everyone experiences at the end of life (Matt. 16:18; Acts 2:27, 31; Rev. 1:18; 6:8; 20:13–14). *Hades* is a temporary location the occupants of which will eventually be cast into the lake of fire after the Great White Throne judgment.
- *Gehenna.* This word is used twelve times in the New Testament and is a term for eternal punishment. The term is derived from the Hebrew word referring to the Valley of Hinnon that runs on the southern and eastern sides of Jerusalem. In Old Testament times, the valley was a place in which pagan worshipers sacrificed infants by fire to the false god Moloch (2 Kings 16:3; 17:7; 21:6). Jeremiah also announced that the valley would be a place of divine judgment (Jer. 7:32; 19:6). In New Testament times, the valley became a place where refuse was continually burned. The imagery of the word would have been very vivid

for the New Testament audience. Therefore, the word became synonymous with eternal punishment and the fires of hell. Its usage describes the eternal punishment associated with the final judgment (Matt. 23:15, 33; 25:41, 46).

- *Tartaros.* This term occurs only in 2 Peter 2:4 and refers to a place where certain, not all, fallen angels (demons) are confined. The word was used in classical mythology for a subterranean abyss in which rebellious gods were punished. The word came over into Hellenistic Judaism and was used also in the apocryphal book of Enoch (2:20) in reference to fallen angels.
- *Other descriptions.* Several other phrases or descriptions of eternal punishment are found in the New Testament, among them *unquenchable fire* (Matt. 3:12; Mark 9:43, 48), *furnace of fire* (Matt. 13:42, 50), *outer darkness* (Matt. 8:12; 22:13; 25:30), *eternal fire* (Matt. 25:41), and *lake of fire* (Rev. 19:20; 20:10, 14–15).

24. Will the punishment be eternal?

According to Revelation 20:11–15, unbelievers will be cast into the lake of fire (hell) after the Great White Throne judgment, and they will remain there for eternity. It is an individual's own choice that brings about this eternal punishment. "Unquestionably the greatest pain suffered by people in hell is that they are forever excluded from the presence of God. If ecstatic joy is found in the presence of God (Ps. 16:11), then utter dismay is found in His absence."[5] Every person must decide if he or she will spend eternity in heaven or in hell. The choice is either eternal punishment or eternal life (Matt. 25:46).

25. What about annihilationism?

Some evangelicals advocate the position of *annihilationism* or *conditional immortality.* Sometimes the terms have different nuances; at other times, they have the same meaning. Gary Habermas and J. P. Moreland note,

> When used differently, conditional immortality is the notion that humans are by nature mortal, God gives the gift of everlasting life to believers, and at death God simply

allows unbelievers to become extinct. Annihilationism often refers to the view that everyone survives death and participates in the final resurrection, but the judgment passed on unbelievers is extinction. Non-Christians undergo everlasting punishment, not everlasting punishing, in that the result of their judgment—annihilation—lasts forever.[6]

We have several arguments against annihilationism, the strongest of which is the fact that many biblical passages refute it.[7] We have noted earlier Jesus' words in Matthew 25:46, "And these will go away into eternal punishment, but the righteous into eternal life." Jesus clearly taught that the consequences of rejecting Him were eternal. Ron Rhodes writes of this passage:

> By no stretch of the imagination can the punishment spoken of in Matthew 25:46 be defined as a nonsuffering extinction of consciousness. Indeed, if actual suffering is lacking, then so is punishment. Let us be clear on this: *punishment entails suffering.* And suffering necessarily entails consciousness. . . . A critical point to make about the punishment described in Matthew 25:46 is that it is said to be *eternal.* There is no way that annihilationism or an extinction of consciousness can be forced into that passage. Indeed, the Greek adjective *aionion* in that verse literally means "everlasting, without end." . . . This same adjective is predicated of God (the "eternal" God) in 1 Timothy 1:17, Romans 16:26, Hebrews 9:14, 13:8, and Revelation 4:9. *The punishment of the wicked is just as eternal as our eternal God.*[8]

26. What about universalism?

Universalism is the concept that all men and women of all ages will ultimately receive salvation and spend eternity in heaven. Universalism has been found in Christianity throughout the centuries, but it has never been considered orthodox, nor has it been widely accepted. Advocates of universalism claim that eternal punishment is inconsistent with a loving God. This view, however, minimizes the justice of God.

Ryrie writes of this theological argument of a loving God:

> Some universalists prefer to argue theologically. They appeal to the nature of God as being totally love. How then, they ask, could such a God condemn anyone either in this life or the life to come? God is too good to reject anyone. However God's character involves not only love and goodness but also righteousness, holiness, and wrath. Universalists sacrifice God's righteousness to His love which results in a god different from the God of the Bible.
>
> Others argue that a just God would not give infinite punishment for finite sin. But this ignores that important principle that crime depends on the object against whom it is committed (an infinite God) as well as on the subject who commits it (finite man). Striking a post is not a culpable act as striking a human being is. All sin is ultimately against an infinite God and deserves infinite punishment.[9]

Ron Rhodes writes of universalism:

> The older form of universalism, originating in the second century, taught that salvation would come after a temporary period of punishment. The newer form of universalism declares that all men *are now* saved, though all do not realize it. Therefore the job of the preacher and the missionary is to tell people they are already saved. Certain Bible passages—John 12:32, Philippians 2:10–11, and 1 Timothy 2:4—are typically twisted out of context in support of universalism.[10]

The Bible is very clear on the fact that not all people will receive salvation and spend eternity in heaven. John 3:18 states, "He who believes in Him is not judged; he who does not believe has been judged already, because he has not believed in the name of the only begotten Son of God." Later in the same chapter we read, "He who believes in the Son has eternal life; but he who does not obey the Son shall not see life, but the wrath of God abides on him" (v. 36).

27. What about reincarnation?

Reincarnation is the nonbiblical view that humans are reborn to earthly existence after their death, and it has always been rejected by Christianity. In the last couple of decades, however, through New Age thought and the influence of Eastern religions, the belief in reincarnation has increased in the United States.

As early as a thousand years before the birth of Christ, reincarnation was first present in Hinduism. Variations of it later appeared in Buddhism. In Western culture, the Greek philosophers, some Roman philosophers, the Gnostics, and some of the Greek mystery religions believed in reincarnation. More recently, it was popularized in the occult movement of Theosophy and through psychics such as Edgar Cayce and Jeane Dixon.

Christianity and the Bible reject any reincarnation. The Bible clearly teaches that we have only one life. Hebrews 9:27 is very straightforward: "It is appointed for men to die once, and after this comes judgment." We also have the words of Jesus to the thief who was crucified beside Him and believed in Him: "Truly I say to you, today you shall be with Me in Paradise" (Luke 23:43). Jesus offered the thief eternal life and immediate entrance into heaven, not reincarnation.

Douglas Connelly summarizes the human condition, the need for salvation, and the mistake of believing in reincarnation:

> Human beings are not progressing upward to God through an endless cycle of rebirths. Instead we are all lost, dead in our sins and separated from the life of God. What redeems us from that dreadful situation is the grace and forgiveness of God, who, because of the atoning sacrifice of Christ on the cross, is free to forgive those who come to him in faith. . . .
>
> Perhaps reincarnation is becoming more widely accepted in Western culture because it is convenient to believe. It is easier to think that you will return to human life again than that you will have to give an account of this life to God, who has the power to cast people into eternal separation from him. Reincarnation also appeals to human pride by teaching

that a person's final destiny rests on human effort, not on the grace or judgment of God. Even human sin is not looked on as something wrong before God but rather as a learning experience, a potential step in a person's upward progress.[11]

How we live this life and where we will spend eternity are the most important issues that every person must decide. This life is not a "dress rehearsal" for another life or for many more lives. You have only one life to live; live it for God.

28. What about the teachings of eternity in other religions?

Only the Bible can provide us with the truths of heaven, and only Christianity offers true glimpses of heaven, eternity, and eternal life. Muslims hold to the concept of an eternal heaven and hell, but it is not the same as the Bible portrays. Hinduism teaches reincarnation and ultimately annihilation. Buddhism emphasizes the concept of nirvana and also a belief in illusory heavens. Judaism stresses a hope of future national salvation. Jesus clearly presented an exclusivist message in John 14:6: "I am the way, and the truth, and the life; no one comes to the Father, but through Me." Only through Jesus Christ can we gain eternal life. Only through the Bible can we gain an accurate knowledge of heaven.

29. What about near-death experiences?

The subject of life after death has been prevalent in our popular culture for the last couple of decades. Some of the interest has been biblically based, but much of it has not. The majority of the popular literature sold and the discussions on radio and television talk shows has been centered in New Age thought, mysticism, Eastern religions, or the occult.

One of the corollaries of this fascination has been the increase and study of near-death experiences (NDE). NDEs have been widely reported, and many people have claimed an experience categorized as an NDE.[12] Biblical evaluations and evangelical responses to the questions surrounding NDEs are also available and should be read by those who have specific questions about NDE.[13] Gary Habermas and J. P. Moreland write of the nature of NDEs that,

We need to make an important distinction between clinical (or reversible) death and biological (or irreversible) death. In clinical death, eternal life signs such as consciousness, pulse, and breathing are absent. In such cases, biological death virtually always results if no steps are taken to reverse the process. Biological death, on the other hand, is not affected by any amount of attention, for it is physically irreversible. . . . Most near-death reports are from those who were close to clinical death.[14]

When considering NDE, it is important to remember that the experience is *not an after-death experience* and therefore cannot provide accurate or legitimate information about the afterlife and heaven. Only the Bible does that. Ron Rhodes writes,

We must keep in mind that near-death experiences do not actually prove anything about the final state of the dead. After all, these experiences are *near-death* experiences, not *once-for-all completely dead* experiences. In fact, as one writer said, near-death experiences "may tell us no more about death than someone who has been near Denver but never within city limits can tell us about that town. Both NDEs (near-Denver and near-death experiences) are bereft of certitude. . . . In both cases, more reliable maps are available."

The map for near-death experiences is, of course, the Bible. Scripture defines death as the separation of the spirit from the body (James 2:26). And true death occurs *only once* (see Heb. 9:27).[15]

The religious content of NDE and its significance for the person who experiences it varies widely and is affected by the worldview of the individual. For example, people with New Age religious beliefs report NDEs consistent with that theology and people with other religious beliefs experience NDEs espousing those views. Habermas and Moreland note that,

It makes sense that the identification of the figure [reli-
gious figures seen in NDEs] will come from the patient's
own background. . . . For instance, no American claimed
to have seen Shiva, Rama, or Krishna. . . . It would ap-
pear, then, that previous religious, cultural, and sociologi-
cal beliefs affect the wide differences in NDE interpretations,
including the way figures are identified. . . . So there are
important reasons that certain factors of interpretation
comment more on a person's beliefs, society, and culture
than they do on the facts themselves.[16]

We must also remember that for some people there may be an
occultic association with the NDE, and it may be of satanic and
demonic origin. Occultic and psychic activities are condemned by
God (Deut. 18:10–13), and any participation or involvement with
them should be shunned. NDE researcher Jerry Yamamoto gives
wise caution regarding NDEs, noting that because they "are of a
subjective nature, determining their source is largely a speculative
venture. With divine, demonic, and several natural factors all mer-
iting considerations, a single, universal explanation for NDEs becomes quite risky."[17]

Discussion about NDEs is interesting, but it doesn't provide any
reliable answers or insights into heaven and eternity, and it has the
potential of demonic deception or leading people far from the
truth of God's Word. Only the Bible can give us infallible information regarding heaven and life after death. Rhodes provides the
following wise counsel on evaluating NDEs:

No matter what kind of experience you have, always test it
against Scripture (see 1 Thess. 5:21). If *anything* contradicts
the Word of God in any way, it must be rejected. *Make the
Scriptures your sole measuring stick.* God's Word will keep you
on track.[18]

PART 5

WHAT IS THE SIGNIFICANCE OF HEAVEN FOR TODAY?

30. Isn't belief in heaven really just escapism?

In Colossians 3:2, Paul exhorts Christians to "set your mind on the things above, not on the things that are on earth." Yet, because Christians have done just as the Bible commanded, they have been accused of escapism. John MacArthur counters this criticism:

> It may sound paradoxical to say this, but heaven should be at the center of the Christian worldview. The term *worldview* has gained great popularity over the past hundred years or so. It describes a moral, philosophical, and spiritual framework through which we interpret the world and everything around us. Everyone *has* a worldview (whether consciously or not).
>
> A proper Christian worldview is uniquely focused heavenward. Though some would deride this as "escapism," it is, after all, the very thing Scripture commands: "Set your affection on things above, not on things on the earth" (Col. 3:2 KJV). The apostle Paul penned that command, and his approach to life was anything but escapist.[1]

Throughout the history of Christianity, the criticism by non-Christians and critics that belief in heaven is really just escapism or a psychological crutch to help people deal with this world has persisted. They argue that heaven isn't real; it's just a coping mechanism. But they are wrong; it's a real hope for Christians who know and experience the trials and tribulations of this world. To believe in heaven does not mean that we ignore this world; it means that we long for a better and eternal world. Joni Eareckson Tada graphically describes this hope:

> I still can hardly believe it. I, with shriveled, bent fingers, atrophied muscles, gnarled knees, and no feeling from the shoulders down, will one day have a new body, light, bright, and clothed in righteousness—powerful and dazzling.
>
> Can you imagine the hope this gives someone spinal-cord injured like me? Or someone who is cerebral palsied, brain-injured, or who has multiple sclerosis? Imagine the hope this gives someone who is manic depressive. No other religion, no other philosophy promises new bodies, hearts, and minds. Only in the Gospel of Christ do hurting people find such incredible hope.[2]

Answering the charge of escapism, Christian philosopher Peter Kreeft writes that the real issue is not escapism, but truth:

> The first and simplest answer to the charge that belief in heaven is escapism is that the first question is not whether it is escapist but whether it is true. We cannot find out whether it is true simply by finding out whether it is escapist. "There is a tunnel under this prison" may be an escapist idea, but it may also be true.
>
> If an idea is true, we want to believe it simply because it is true, whether it is escapist or not. If it is false, we want to reject it simply because it is false, whether it is escapist or not. The only honest reason for anyone ever accepting any idea is its truth.[3]

The truths about heaven are not escapist, but they are inescapable. "Thinking about heaven is not escapism because it determines my essence. . . . Finding my purpose is the exact opposite of escapism; it is finding my essence."[4]

31. What about the sorrow and grief we experience now in this world?

Christians and non-Christians alike suffer hardships, endure pain, lose loved ones, and grieve. But for the Christian there is eternal hope because of the faith placed in the person and work of Jesus Christ. Because of this fact, Paul, who himself endured many hardships and afflictions, was able to say, "For to me, to live is Christ, and to die is gain" (Phil. 1:21).

In Psalm 56:8, David says, "Thou hast taken account of my wanderings; put my tears in Thy bottle; are they not in Thy book?" God is very aware of our sighs and cries, our tears and fears, and one day He will wipe them all away. For Christians, the grief and sorrow that we experience is real and natural, but it is also temporary. That is one of the reasons why Paul provides the Thessalonians with the encouragement of 1 Thessalonians 4:13–18 and the teaching on the Rapture:

> But we do not want you to be uninformed, brethren, about those who are asleep, that you may not grieve, as do the rest who have no hope. For if we believe that Jesus died and rose again, even so God will bring with Him those who have fallen asleep in Jesus. For this we say to you by the word of the Lord, that we who are alive, and remain until the coming of the Lord, shall not precede those who have fallen asleep. For the Lord Himself will descend from heaven with a shout, with the voice of the archangel, and with the trumpet of God; and the dead in Christ shall rise first. Then we who are alive and remain shall be caught up together with them in the clouds to meet the Lord in the air, and thus we shall always be with the Lord. Therefore comfort one another with these words.

In Revelation 21:4, John tells us that one day God "shall wipe away every tear from their eyes; and there shall no longer be any death; there shall no longer be any mourning, or crying, or pain; the first things have passed away." What we experience on earth is real, but what we experience in heaven will also be real.

Heaven will be a place where

- there is no more pain,
- there is no more suffering,
- there are no more hardships,
- there are no more tears, and
- there is no more death.

For those who long for heaven, it is like the words in the spiritual, "All my trials, Lord, soon be over." Heaven means healing. Heaven means hope. Heaven means home.

32. Why should I be concerned about heaven?

"Pie in the sky by and by" is the frequent accusation and attitude of those who deny the present application of the truth of heaven. But belief in and knowledge of heaven matters very much and has daily ramifications. We should be concerned about heaven because it pertains to our eternal destiny. For the Christian, it also is an impetus for godly living, evangelism, and daily ministry to others. Joni Eareckson Tada writes of the daily significance of heaven:

> When a Christian realizes his citizenship is in heaven, he begins acting as a responsible citizen of earth. He invests wisely in relationships because he knows they're eternal. His conversations, goals, and motives become pure and honest because he realizes these will have a bearing on everlasting reward. He gives generously of time, money, and talent because he's laying up treasure for eternity. He spreads the good news of Christ because he longs to fill heaven's ranks with his friends and neighbors. All this serves the pilgrim well not only in heaven, but on earth; for it serves everyone around him.[5]

Heaven does matter today. It is a reminder that life will not always continue as it does today (2 Peter 3:2–7). Things will change, and our lives will pass. Sometimes we forget or ignore that fact.

We really don't believe it's all going to end, do we? If God hadn't told us differently, we'd all think this parade of life would go on forever.

But it will end. This life is not forever, nor is it the best life that will ever be. The fact is that believers *are* headed for heaven. It is a reality. And what we do here on earth has a direct bearing on how we live there. Heaven may be as near as next year, or next week; so it makes good sense to spend some time here on earth thinking candid thoughts about that marvelous future reserved for us.[6]

In Romans 8:22–23, Paul writes,

For we know that the whole creation groans and suffers the pains of childbirth together until now. And not only this, but also we ourselves, having the first fruits of the Spirit, even we ourselves groan within ourselves, waiting eagerly for our adoption as sons, the redemption of our body.

The body of which Paul speaks is the resurrection body that Christians will have in heaven, but the longings are those of this world. John MacArthur expresses this well:

Although sin has crippled our souls and marred our spirits—though it has scarred our thoughts, wills, and emotions—we who know Christ have already had a taste of what redemption is like. And so we long for that day when we will be completely redeemed. We yearn to reach that place where the seed of perfection that has been planted within us will bloom into fullness and we will be completely redeemed, finally made perfect (Heb. 12:22–23). That is exactly what heaven is all about.[7]

For many questions about heaven the Bible does not provide either clear answers or any answers. For some concerns, we must rely on theological deduction or consider the silence of Scripture. God has told us what we need to know, not all of what we want to know. Many things we do know, as we see in the preceding pages, but there is definitely more silence than we would like.

> But we must also remember that there is far, far more we *don't* know about heaven than we do know; its beauties and glories are literally inconceivable to us now. We should expect nothing less from a future kingdom prepared by Jesus, Himself, for those He loves and died for (Matt. 25:34; John 14:2). Apart from Christ, there is no such thing as *real* life—now or forever.[8]

33. How can I be sure I'll go to heaven?

Theologian Carl F. H. Henry has said of contemporary society and its citizens, "The intellectual suppression of God in His revelation has precipitated the bankruptcy of a civilization that turned its back on heaven only to make its bed in hell."[9] Is this bold but true statement an accurate reflection of your own spiritual status?

Perhaps you have reached this final question in this booklet and yet do not know for sure what your eternal destiny will be. If so, then this is the most important question of the booklet for you, and we encourage you to consider carefully its contents.

We would like you to know for sure that you have eternal life through Jesus Christ, God's Son. In Revelation, the closing book of the Bible, John issues a last invitation: "And the Spirit and the bride say, 'Come.' And let the one who hears say, 'Come.' And let the one who is thirsty come; let the one who wishes take the water of life without cost" (Rev. 22:17). What does this invitation mean?

The image is that of a wedding. The groom has issued an invitation to the bride. The groom is willing, but is the bride willing? In this same way, God has made provision for you—at no expense to you, but at great expense to Him—to enter into a relationship with Him that will give you eternal life. More specifically, the invitation is issued to the one who hears and who is thirsty. *Thirst* represents a need: forgiveness of sin. Thus, you must recognize that you are a sinner in the eyes of God: "For all have sinned and fall short of the glory of God" (Rom. 3:23). God is holy and thus cannot ignore anyone's sin. He must judge it. However, God in His mercy has provided a way by which sinful men and women can receive His forgiveness. This forgiveness was provided at a great cost by Jesus Christ when He came to earth two thousand years ago, lived a perfect life, and died on the cross in our place to pay for our sin: "For the wages of sin is death, but the free gift of God is eternal life in Jesus Christ our Lord" (Rom. 6:23). The Bible also says, "Christ died for our sins according to the Scriptures, and that He was buried, and that He was raised on the third day according to the Scriptures" (1 Cor. 15:3-4).

To obtain this salvation and the eternal life that Jesus Christ offers, we must individually trust that Christ's payment through His death on the cross is the only way that we can receive the forgiveness of our sins, the re-establishment of a relationship with God, and eternal life. "For by grace you have been saved through faith; and that not of yourselves, it is the gift of God; not as a result of works, that no one should boast" (Eph. 2:8-9). This is why John invites the thirsty to come and enter into a relationship with God through Christ.

Are you thirsty? Do you recognize your sin before God? If you do, then come to Christ. If you do not acknowledge your need for salvation, then you bypass this opportunity. Please don't.

Those who are thirsty and want salvation can express their trust through the following prayer:

> Dear Lord, I know that I have done wrong and fallen short of Your perfect ways. I realize that my sins have separated me from You and that I deserve Your judgment. I believe that You sent Your Son, Jesus Christ, to earth to die on the cross for my sins. I put my trust in Jesus Christ and what He did on the cross as payment for my sins. Please forgive me and give me eternal life. Amen.

If you just prayed this prayer in sincerity, you are now a child of God and have eternal life. Heaven will be your eternal home. Welcome to the family of God! As His child, you will want to develop this wonderful relationship by learning more about God through study of the Bible. You will want to find a church that teaches

God's Word, encourages fellowship with other believers, and promotes the spreading of God's message of forgiveness to others.

If you were a Christian before reading this booklet, we encourage you to continue in your relationship with Christ. As you grow, you will want to live for Him in light of His coming. You will want to continue to spread the message of forgiveness that you have experienced. As you see God setting the stage for the end-time drama of events, you should be motivated to increased service until He comes. May your heart be occupied with His words:

> Behold, I am coming quickly, and My reward is with Me, to render to every man according to what he has done. I am the Alpha and the Omega, the first and the last, the beginning and the end." Blessed are those who wash their robes, that they may have the right to the tree of life, and may enter by the gates into the city. (Revelation 22:12–14)

CONCLUSION

C. S. Lewis once remarked about spiritual matters and our frequent preoccupation with worldly concerns that "all that is not eternal is eternally out of date."[1] We live and die in a fast-moving world. Everywhere we turn or go, people, including ourselves, are busy. But are we busy doing the right things? Or are we so focused on the present and, at times, the past, that we miss or neglect the future? Gary Habermas and J. P. Moreland have written of heaven,

> The God of the universe invites us to view life and death from His eternal vantage point. And if we do, we will see how readily it can revolutionize our lives: daily anxieties, emotional hurts, tragedies, our responses and responsibilities to others, possessions, wealth, and even physical pain and death. All of this and much more can be informed and influenced by the truths of heaven. The repeated witness of the New Testament is that believers should view all problems, indeed, their entire existence, from what we call the "top-down" perspective: God and His kingdom first, followed by various aspects of our earthly existence.[2]

Heaven is indeed a unique and wonderful place, a location that far exceeds our imagination and comprehension. For the Christian, it is a present hope and eternal home. "Heaven is a realm of inexpressible glory."[3] The decision you make about heaven and the free offer of salvation based on the death of Jesus Christ is the most important decision you will ever make. Take care of your soul; you will have it for eternity.

NOTES

Introduction

1. C. S. Lewis, *Mere Christianity* (New York: Simon and Schuster, 1996), 119 (Book III, Ch. 10).
2. Steven J. Lawson, *Heaven Help Us! Truths About Eternity That Will Help You Live Today* (Colorado Springs: NavPress, 1995), 16.

Part 1: What Is Heaven?

1. For examples from classical literature, see Wilbur M. Smith, *The Biblical Doctrine of Heaven* (Chicago: Moody, 1968), 28–29.
2. John F. MacArthur, *The Glory of Heaven* (Wheaton, Ill.: Crossway, 1996), 56.
3. Ibid., 59–60.
4. Ibid., 60.
5. Gary R. Habermas and J. P. Moreland, *Immortality: The Other Side of Death* (Nashville: Nelson, 1992), 150.
6. Arnold G. Fruchtenbaum, *Footsteps of the Messiah: A Study of the Sequence of Prophetic Events* (Tustin, Calif.: Ariel Ministries, 1982), 366.
7. For a fuller discussion of Jerusalem by the authors, see *The Truth About Jerusalem in Bible Prophecy* (Eugene, Ore.: Harvest House, 1996).
8. John F. Walvoord, *Major Bible Prophecies: 37 Crucial Prophecies That Affect You Today* (Grand Rapids: Zondervan, 1991), 404.
9. Charles C. Ryrie, *Basic Theology* (Wheaton, Ill.: Victor, 1986), 515.
10. The chart is taken from Ryrie, *Basic Theology*, 516, and used with the permission of the publisher.

Part 2: What Will Heaven Be Like?

1. See Wilbur M. Smith, *The Biblical Doctrine of Heaven* (Chicago: Moody, 1968), 190–200; Don Baker, *Heaven: A Glimpse of Your Future Home* (Portland, Ore.: Multnomah, 1983); and Douglas Connelly, *After Life: What the Bible Really Says* (Downers Grove, Ill.: InterVarsity, 1995), 101–3.
2. Smith, *Biblical Doctrine of Heaven,* 190.
3. Baker, *Heaven,* n.p.
4. Steven J. Lawson, *Heaven Help Us! Truths About Eternity That Will Help You Live Today* (Colorado Springs: NavPress, 1995), 52–66.
5. Baker, *Heaven,* n.p.
6. Ibid.
7. Joni Eareckson Tada, *Heaven: Your Real Home* (Grand Rapids: Zondervan, 1995), 39.
8. John F. MacArthur, *The Glory of Heaven* (Wheaton, Ill.: Crossway, 1996), 133.
9. Ibid., 139.
10. Ibid., 136.
11. Charles C. Ryrie, *Basic Theology* (Wheaton, Ill.: Victor, 1986), 121–22.

Part 3: Who Will Be in Heaven?

1. John F. MacArthur, *The Glory of Heaven* (Wheaton, Ill.: Crossway, 1996), 129.
2. This material is summarized from Gary R. Habermas and J. P. Moreland, *Immortality: The Other Side of Death* (Nashville: Nelson, 1992), 114.
3. Ken Gire, *Instructive Moments with the Savior* (Grand Rapids: Zondervan, 1992), 75.
4. Ron Rhodes, *The Undiscovered Country* (Eugene, Ore.: Harvest House, 1996), 102. Rhodes provides an excellent discussion of this topic and many of the other issues related to heaven. His work is highly recommended.
5. Ibid., 101.
6. Ibid., 101–2.
7. Ibid., 107.
8. Ibid., 108, 205 n. 12.

9. Robert Lightner, *Heaven for Those Who Can't Believe* (Schaumburg, Ill.: Regular Baptist Press, 1977), 22.

10. Steven J. Lawson, *Heaven Help Us! Truths About Eternity That Will Help You Live Today* (Colorado Springs: NavPress, 1995), 81.

11. MacArthur, *Glory of Heaven,* 142.

Part 4: What Does the Future Hold for Non-Christians?

1. For a complete study of the issue, see Ramesh P. Richard, *The Population of Heaven* (Chicago: Moody, 1994).

2. Cited in John Ankerberg and John Weldon, *The Facts on Life After Death* (Eugene, Ore.: Harvest House, 1992), 41.

3. C. S. Lewis, *The Great Divorce* (New York: Macmillan, 1946), 69.

4. Gary R. Habermas and J. P. Moreland, *Immortality: The Other Side of Death* (Nashville: Nelson, 1992), 159.

5. Ron Rhodes, *The Undiscovered Country* (Eugene, Ore.: Harvest House, 1996), 118.

6. Habermas and Moreland, *Immortality,* 169.

7. Ibid., 169–76. See also William Crockett, *Four Views on Hell* (Grand Rapids: Zondervan, 1992), for a "pro and con" treatment of all of the major views regarding hell.

8. Rhodes, *Undiscovered Country,* 121–23.

9. Charles C. Ryrie, *Basic Theology* (Wheaton, Ill.: Victor, 1986), 521.

10. Rhodes, *Undiscovered Country,* 122–23.

11. Douglas Connelly, *After Life: What the Bible Really Says* (Downers Grove, Ill.: InterVarsity, 1995), 44–45.

12. Ankerberg and Weldon, *Facts on Life After Death,* 9. See also Habermas and Moreland, *Immortality,* 87; and Rhodes, *Undiscovered Country,* 149.

13. See especially Habermas and Moreland, *Immortality,* 73–105; Rhodes, *Undiscovered Country,* 149–67; Ankerberg and Weldon, *Facts on Life After Death;* and John Ankerberg and John Weldon, *The Facts on Near-Death Experiences* (Eugene, Ore.: Harvest House, 1996). For a biblical critique of Betty J. Eadie's popular but unbiblical *Embraced by the Light* (Thorndike, Mass.: G. K. Hall, 1993) see Doug Groothius, *Deceived by the Light* (Eugene, Ore.: Harvest House, 1995).

14. Habermas and Moreland, *Immortality*, 73.
15. Rhodes, *Undiscovered Country*, 164.
16. Habermas and Moreland, *Immortality*, 91–92.
17. Jerry Yamamoto, "The Near-Death Experience," *Christian Research Journal* (spring 1992): 5.
18. Rhodes, *Undiscovered Country*, 167.

Part 5: What Is the Significance of Heaven for Today?
1. John F. MacArthur, *The Glory of Heaven* (Wheaton, Ill.: Crossway, 1996), 50.
2. Joni Eareckson Tada, *Heaven: Your Real Home* (Grand Rapids: Zondervan, 1995), 53.
3. Peter Kreeft, *Heaven: The Heart's Deepest Longing* (San Francisco: Ignatius Press, 1989), 164.
4. Ibid., 170.
5. Tada, *Heaven*, 110.
6. Ibid., 15.
7. MacArthur, *Glory of Heaven*, 123.
8. John Ankerberg and John Weldon, *The Facts on Near-Death Experiences* (Eugene, Ore.: Harvest House, 1996), 40.
9. Carl F. H. Henry, *Twilight of a Great Civilization* (Westchester, Ill.: Crossway Books, 1988), 143.

Conclusion
1. C. S. Lewis, *The Four Loves* (New York: Harcourt Brace Jovanovich, 1960), 188 (Ch. VI).
2. Gary R. Habermas and J. P. Moreland, *Immortality: The Other Side of Death* (Nashville: Nelson, 1992), 186.
3. John F. MacArthur, *The Glory of Heaven* (Wheaton, Ill.: Crossway, 1996), 81.

RECOMMENDED READING

Ankerberg, John, and John Weldon. *The Facts on Angels.* Eugene, Ore.: Harvest House, 1995.

———. *The Facts on Life After Death.* Eugene, Ore.: Harvest House, 1992.

———. *The Facts on Near-Death Experiences.* Eugene, Ore.: Harvest House, 1996.

Baker, Don. *Heaven: A Glimpse of Your Future Home.* Portland, Ore.: Multnomah, 1983.

Benware, Paul N. *Understanding End Times Prophecy: A Comprehensive Approach.* Chicago: Moody, 1995.

Connelly, Douglas. *After Life: What the Bible Really Says.* Downers Grove, Ill.: InterVarsity, 1995.

Crockett, William. *Four Views on Hell.* Grand Rapids: Zondervan, 1992.

Habermas, Gary, and J. P. Moreland. *Immortality: The Other Side of Death.* Nashville: Nelson, 1992.

Jeffrey, Grant R. *Heaven: The Last Frontier.* Toronto: Frontier Research, 1990.

Lawson, Steven J. *Heaven Help Us!* Colorado Springs: NavPress, 1995.

Lightner, Robert. *Heaven for Those Who Can't Believe.* Schaumburg, Ill.: Regular Baptist Press, 1977.

MacArthur, John F. *The Glory of Heaven.* Wheaton, Ill.: Crossway Books, 1996.

Martindale, Wayne, ed. *Journey to the Celestial City.* Chicago: Moody, 1995.

Rhodes, Ron. *Angels Among Us.* Eugene, Ore.: Harvest House, 1994.

———. *The Undiscovered Country.* Eugene, Ore.: Harvest House, 1996.

Richard, Ramesh P. *The Population of Heaven.* Chicago: Moody, 1984.

Ryrie, Charles C. *Basic Theology.* Wheaton, Ill.: Victor Books, 1986.

Smith, Wilbur M. *The Biblical Doctrine of Heaven.* Chicago: Moody, 1968.

Stowell, Joseph M. *Eternity.* Chicago: Moody, 1995.

Tada, Joni Eareckson. *Heaven: Your Real Home.* Grand Rapids: Zondervan, 1995.

Walvoord, John F. *Major Bible Prophecies: 37 Crucial Prophecies That Affect You Today.* Grand Rapids: Zondervan, 1991.

——. *The Millennial Kingdom.* Findlay, Ohio: Dunham, 1959.